Three Paws' Christmas Wish

Book 5

KAREN STRUCK

♡ Karen Struck

PAGE PUBLISHING
Conneaut Lake, PA

First originally published by Page Publishing 2022

ISBN 978-1-6624-7834-5 (pbk)
ISBN 978-1-6624-7835-2 (hc)
ISBN 978-1-6624-7836-9 (digital)

Printed in the United States of America

Dedication

"You can find magic
wherever you look.
Sit back and relax,
all you need is a book."

Dr. Seuss

The entire Three Paws series is dedicated to my talented illustrator who has brought life to my wilderness friends.

~ Thank you so much ~

"Today is the big reveal!" said Dr. Noah as he and vet tech Tracy slid open the window into Boots's transparent enclosure.

It's been two months since Boots saved Pepe the iguana from being crushed by a falling slab of stone during the October earthquake. He was sent to Dr. Noah's Hospital of Hope to recover.

Christmas is only a week away, thought Boots. *Surely Dr. Noah will let me return to my friends and family before Christmas.*

He stared at the white cast covering his left paw. Boots felt a tiny sting on his neck and soon felt very sleepy. Tracy darted him with a shot of sleeping medication, so they could safely remove his cast. When Boots awakened, the cast was gone.

"Amazing!" he said. "My Christmas wish has come true. My new paw is perfect!" He had only to *think* of a command, and his mechanical paw would move as he desired.

Sockeye, Chinook, and Goose approached the enclosure. Goose carried on his back Pepe and Pepe's new girlfriend, Sora. Both iguanas were dressed in fur from head to toe.

Goose and his sister, Sora—a blue iguana—invited Pepe to live with them after the earthquake.

Pepe and Sora fell in love—quite an annoyance to Goose because Pepe was *his* little buddy. Now the three were inseparable.

"Time to celebrate the holidays," cheered Sockeye and Chinook.

As the friends laughed and joked together, Dr. Noah and Tracy approached the front of Boots's enclosure. The wilderness friends quickly hid behind the snowy evergreen trees.

"I have exciting news for our special bear," said Dr. Noah. He pointed to a large van in the parking lot labeled *San Diego Zoo.* "Our bionic bear, with his mechanical paw, is going to be flown to the San Diego Zoo the day after Christmas. He'll be their featured exhibit!"

"No!" gasped Sockeye.

When Dr. Noah and Tracy left, the friends returned shocked by the news.

"How can he do this to me?" asked Boots in disbelief. His world was about to change forever.

Pepe walked toward Boots, removed his sombrero, and slid it through the small opening just above the lock to the enclosure. "I think you need my sombrero more than I do."

Feeling a bit awkward, Boots reached for the sombrero. He placed the tiny hat—the size of a thimble—on his big furry head and thought, *Maybe Pepe's sombrero really does have magical powers.*

Pepe suddenly had a mischievous twinkle in his eyes. "I've got a plan!" he said.

"It's risky, but we have no other options."

Sockeye stood tall and placed her paws against the glass. "Have faith, Boots. We're all in this together."

As the sun faded to darkness, Boots gazed upon the glowing stars and smiled at the constellation of stars known as Capricornus: half-goat-half fish. He thought of his heavenly friend, Cappy the goat, and whispered, "I need a miracle, Cappy," as if the stars were magical. Boots longed to be with his family. He reminisced about his life since he was a cub.

He remembered going into the river as a young cub and injuring his paw after plunging down a waterfall.

He remembered Cappy falling down the mountainside to the river's edge where their friendship began. Boots helped his injured friend back up the mountain and, in return, Cappy taught him how to catch salmon with only three paws.

He remembered the day he met Sockeye and Pepe under the Sitka tree. Sockeye taught him how to climb trees to escape predators.

He remembered helping Scarlet say goodbye to her grandfather, Cappy.

He remembered the fun times whitewater rafting with his friends.

Most importantly, he remembered the October earthquake where they almost lost Pepe.

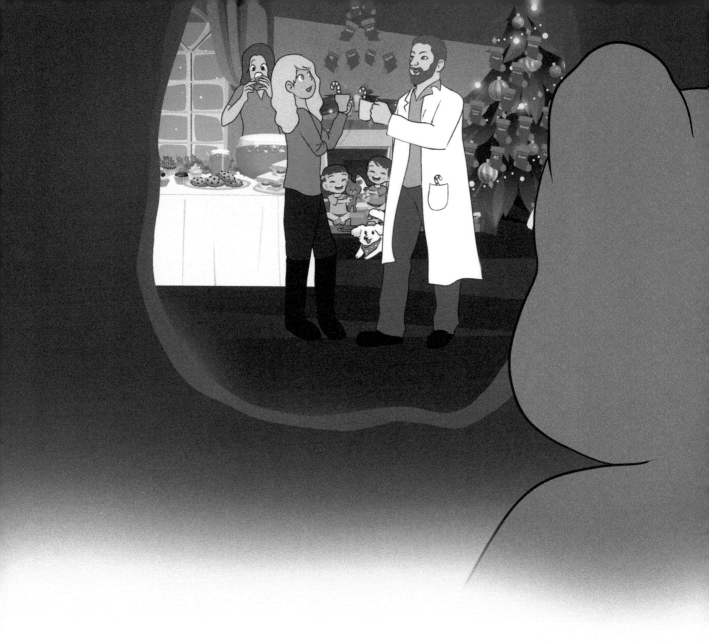

As the days passed, Boots continued to pray for a miracle. It was Christmas Eve. *Dr. Noah has no right to send me away and keep me in a cage.* Boots heard Christmas music playing, glasses clinking, children laughing, and everyone celebrating with their friends and family. Not Boots. He was alone on Christmas Eve.

Back at the den, the wilderness friends were ready to put their plan into action.

"Midnight. Time to act," said Pepe.

Dr. Noah and Ranger Rylee were exiting the hospital when they noticed a flurry of eagles flying in a rhythmic pattern, dancing amidst the Aurora Borealis—the northern lights in the sky.

"How strange!" said Dr. Noah, looking puzzled. "Is that a…*happy face*…made of… *eagles?*"

15

While the eagles distracted the humans, the wilderness friends were busy too. In keeping with the Christmas spirit, Pepe and Sora were dressed as Santa and Mrs. Claus. Goose was a Christmas elf.

"Feliz Navidad!" laughed Pepe, reaching into his Santa bag and pulling out a thin metal piece with a curved end. "This should do it!" he said as he quickly picked the lock to Boots' enclosure.

Click, click, click, and the door opened.

"Hooray!" They all clapped, not realizing they set off an alarm.

Goose yelled, "RUN!"

Dr. Noah and Ranger Rylee saw Boots escaping, surprised by his unusual group of friends.

Ranger Rylee quickly grasped Dr. Noah's forearm, preventing him from calling security.

"Let him live his life where he belongs…not in a cage…but in the beauty that surrounds us."

Dr. Noah admitted, "*Alaska* is his home."

Back at the den, friends and family prepared a celebratory campfire near the river's edge, creating warmth amid the twinkling Christmas lights.

Boots felt a hard lump in his throat as he took center stage.

He raised his arms toward the sky and shouted, "*Freedom,* my friends, is the greatest gift of all. MERRY CHRISTMAS!"

21

Six months later…

Boots and Sockeye welcomed three young cubs into their wilderness family.

Pepe made three little sombreros for the cubs just as his Abuela made for him. Angel wings will cover and protect the cubs as they pursue their dreams one adventure at a time.

The End

About the Author

The magic of Christmas lives within each one of us. It is a time to enjoy Christmas traditions like baking holiday cookies, decorating the house, listening to Christmas music, and spending extra time with friends and family. The true spirit of Christmas is a time for giving. Think of a special way to bring happiness to someone who may need some extra Christmas cheer to help them through the holidays. Anything is possible with a little Christmas magic.

Christmas in Alaska is a wonder to behold.
With Boots and friends together again,
they have found their pot of gold.
Their bond of friendship is one to cherish
like a fairy tale of olde.
They laugh and play throughout the day,
they don't even mind the cold.
The wilderness friends, together again,
full of Christmas cheer,
they love one another like it's Christmas day
every day of the year.

Karen Struck

According to Walt Disney, "All our dreams come true, if we have the courage to pursue them." May all of your wishes, desires, and dreams come true.

MERRY CHRISTMAS!

CPSIA information can be obtained
at www.ICGtesting.com
Printed in the USA
BVHW020008201022
649128BV00001B/6